MARKETING
MANAGEMENT

Table of Contents

UNIT 1
INTRODUCTION TO MODERN MARKETING METHODS

Even though marketing can be seen virtually everywhere an individual looks today, its overall description and application could be confusing to people who want to know what marketing really is. Since there are so many different ways to provide marketing services, each company can have its own distinct concepts that it would use to define its marketing plans. Because the competition in most industries are stiff and the game can be played by anyone who throws in his hat, companies are hiring whole marketing teams to deploy strategies that could be pushed aggressively throughout the entire company.

Marketing can be described in a wide diversity of ways. However, the basic concept of marketing is considered to be the activities an individual or an organization undertake to communicate the actual value of a service or a product to consumers, specifically for the purposes of making a sale. Since technology has had a great impact on how marketing in a company is done, there are many new approaches being used today. Some of the more popular are based on social media strategies that cater to specific target audiences.

Overview of Traditional Approaches to Marketing

Before discussing the latest and most recent innovations in this area, it is important to provide a brief overview of earlier approaches that have been used to increase a company's bottom line. Starting with the 1960s, marketing specialists placed most or all of their efforts on producing high volumes of products and services in order to meet the customer's demands head on. Additionally, similar to sales orientation methods, marketing specialists exploited economies of scale to lower the price that each unit would cost their customer.

In the 1960s, however, marketing campaigns changed dramatically. They morphed into manufacturing teams and marketing specialists who would concentrate on the quality of the products made. This meant that the primary objective for that time was: produce great quality products and the customers would automatically come. While this concept was completely logical to deploy, one of the downsides to this concept was the shift in consumer taste, especially since this could change swiftly with little to no notice. In some scenarios, these shifts were often controlled by present needs and by marketing specialists who created their own demand for a product. This demand was accomplished by developing unique marketing schemes that worked for specific target audiences.

The 1970s to Present Marketing Schemes

This said, from the 1970s to present, the selling methods have changed dramatically in the industry. The overall change in strategy involves the primary focus being customer orientation. Henceforth, marketing consumer goods and services became based solely on their customers' needs and taste. In order to accomplish these goals and objectives, however, marketing specialists must be able to anticipate consumer demand in advance. Some of the measurements used in finding out this kind of information is normally done through research, surveys, and other communication vehicles that could assist in extracting this information from one or more target audiences. Regardless of the type of product or service that the consumer is looking for, the company and its marketing department will have to use their skills and experience acquired over the years to maximize profits.

Marketing Campaigns and Innovations in Technology.

It's not uncommon for today's marketers use a wide diversity of marketing campaigns to sell products. Since the advent of the Internet, a wide door of opportunities has opened to broaden a target audience and to encompass groups around the world. In order to do this successfully, however, marketing managers and their teams must be in sync with the latest changes in the industry. This allows whole teams to deploy a marketing strategy that could be seen across a diversity of platforms (i.e laptops, desktop computers, mobile devices, etc). For instance, many companies can run an ad that would appeal to a specific target audience. For example, people who have their own mobile phones could use this device to purchase different kinds of products, in real time. From buying a television from a popular brand name electronic company to purchasing discounted toner for a picture, it is important to note that there are different innovations that can impact the entire company.

In addition to using the internet to advertise products, marketing teams could also take advantage of campaigns that involve online marketing ads. When done right, the team will have access to large groups at a time to sell different types of products that would maximize the profits.

Also, once a specific social media group has been identified for an ad campaign, marketing specialists can send communication to consumers about new and existing products that they want to sell in large quantities. This is often done by building up the company's brand in the mind of the consumer via campaigns sent via twitter, Facebook, and other major media groups in the industry. While there are pros and cons to reaching consumers via social media strategies, the biggest advantage is reaching large groups at once. This allows a product or service to go viral within minutes.

Marketing can be described in many different ways today, even though the ultimate goal and objectives are the same. From selling goods and services to consumers via a social media forum to sending coupons on a mobile phone, the face of marketing could vary from one marketing campaign to another. Traditional campaigns in the past focused on developing quality products only, which meant that consumers would automatically purchase the newer product. Today's marketing specialists, however, are now positioned to develop campaigns that are based on customer orientation. Which means, the consumer drives the manufacturing process, depending on their needs and desires.

UNIT 2
BUILDING YOUR NETWORK

Networking is a continuing process of identifying individuals that can have a positive influence on your business. Creating a successful network takes time and resources, but it is well worth the venture for start-up enterprises.

If you are a business insider, having worked as an employee of an enterprise that produces your product or makes your service, you have a good head start. You may already have a better understanding of the background in which you will be working. You may even have advanced relationships that you can take advantage of when you decide to leave your current job to go out on your own.

If you are not presently employed in the industry you plan to work in, you would likely have an idea of how the trade functions and who the key actors are. In either case, it is important to stay connected. Attend industry symposiums and trade shows, join trade groups, exchange with others about your business. By placing yourself at events and locations visited by industry insiders you will not only learn what occupational tools and processes are common in the trade, you would also gain valuable contacts. Exchange business cards with other specialists in the field; they may be future clientele or partners.

Once you create networks, fostering these relations could involve an act as easy as having a friendly conversation at a trade display or returning a vendor's phone call. Also remember, the persons in your network also have other networks. Here is a simple example. Just after beginning his business, a client entering the plant nursery trade held a sale at his house and exhibited some plants. A keen neighbor came to the sale, admired the plants and asked a small number of gardening questions. He didn't buy anything, but a few weeks later, his mother called to order trees for a large landscaping project.

Networking works better when it is affordable. If your business doesn't have a large budget for marketing, networking provides a low-cost alternative for raising your profile in the market. Many organized networking events, such as those involving business associations, schools, and networking clubs are either free or have minimal fees. Talking with a potential client, dealer or business associate costs nothing but a little of your time. The potential to produce positive leads and referrals is well worth the effort it takes to participate in meaningful networking opportunities.

To attain success through networking here are a few simple tips.

- Always showcase yourself in a professional manner. While a lot of networking events involve social activities, remember, you are a representative of your business. Dress appropriately for the occasion, be ready to discuss your business in a welcoming manner, and listen with attention as other participants share their business thoughts.

- Be a resource to your associates/ contacts. If you share info with your contacts and help them over their professional hurdles, they are more probable to do the same for you or someone else. You do not need to exchange proprietary information. Simply offer guidelines, suggestions and stories could go a long way toward building a mutually beneficial working relationship.
- Always be on the lookout for fresh networking opportunities. An exchange in a coffee shop or on the bus could lead to new trade. Carry your business cards and exchange them with anyone who shows interest in your business or service.
- Organize your contact info for easy access. Your network will increase as your enterprise grows. By storing addresses or business cards on your laptop or in an adequate filing system, you could retrieve discover contact information quickly. When possible, enter personal information about each contact next to their contact info. For example, write down where you met the contact or jot down some key items you discussed with them. Not only will this keep the person fresh in your mind, it would also help you direct future conversations.
- Networking opens opportunities. All, it takes to build a successful network, is an understanding of your industry.

How Does Network Marketing Work?

Online marketing works on the simple concept of helping each member grow his/her trade profitably. Network marketers endorse the businesses of their affiliates, attaining customers for their businesses. This act is then reciprocated.

Tips on How to Get Network Marketing Work for You!

It's important to find the right network. You will be more proactive in promoting a business that you consider interesting and practical. You can effortlessly build your network when you like what you are doing. This would enable you to pour your time, devotion, and efforts passionately towards growing your network.

You should see yourself not just a normal marketer who promotes products or services, but rather as a business owner who wants to exchange the business experience with others so that everyone could benefit financially. You see, a network marketer contrasts with an ordinary salesperson, as the former is more enthusiastic about his products or services than the latter.

UNIT 3
MARKET PLAN

Firms and people who have become successful in marketing started with a marketing plan. Big companies have plans with hundreds of pages while small companies can get moving with a half- dozen sheets. It's good to put your marketing plan in a three-ring binder and refer to it at least quarterly, but better still, monthly. Have a tab for uploading monthly reports on manufacturing/sales as this would allow you to keep track of your performance as you follow the plan. The plan should actually cover one year. For small firms this is often the best way to think about marketing. People leave, things change, and customers come and go. Give yourself some time to create a plan even if it's just few pages. Coming up with a plan is the 'heavy lifting' of the marketing. While executing your plan, there may surface several obstacles, Therefore, deciding what to do and how to do is the greatest t challenge. Remember all the players in the company should see the plan. Below are steps on how to create a marketing plan.

#1: The executive summary

This includes a high level summary of the whole marketing plan and, paradoxically, the last section that you should write. It's good to have a brief executive summary that sums up everything. When documenting the executive summary, imagine that you are going to present it in an "elevator style" pitch. Once you are done, read it loudly. If this takes you more than ten seconds to do, then you should try to simplify it.

#2: The challenge

This part should have a brief description of the products/services that your company offers. Include the goals (strategic goals, sales figures and company goals) that you want to set for each product. Keep the number of your goals to three at most and let them be measurable, concise and moderately easy to achieve.

#3: Situation analysis

This section should have your customer base, a snapshot of your company and your market at large. It needs to be sub - divided into six sections including:

Company analysis

- Company estimated market share
- Short term and long term company goal
- The strength of the company
- The focus of the company which should be in line with vision and missing statement.
- Analysis of the culture of the company
- Weaknesses of the company

Customer analysis

- Estimate the size of your customer base

- Value drivers
- The main demographics of your customer base

Competitor analysis

- Strengths
- Weaknesses
- Market position
- Collaborators
- Companies and people that are key to what you are doing i.e. suppliers, joint ventures, distributor s, subsidiaries etc.

Climate

- This can be done using the PEST analysis.
- Political and legal environment
- Economic environment
- Social and cultural environment
- Technological environment

SWOT analysis

- Internal strength of your company
- Internal weaknesses of your company
- External opportunities for your company
- External threats to your company

#4: Market segmentation

Every market has its own different segments. Understanding well the relevant segments for your product is always important. Segments should be accessible, measurable, durable, large enough to produce profits and different from other segments.

#5: Alternative marketing strategies

Jot down the details of the previous and alternate strategies that you had with your team before agreeing on the current strategy. These may include changing the price of certain product or eliminating a product

#6: Selected marketing strategy

Give an explanation of the strategy that you and your team have developed and agreed upon. Give reason on why you feel that it's the best strategy for the near future and why you chose that strategy. Once in done in paper put your 4 p's in very product as follows:

Product

- Brand name
- Quality of the product
- Scope of the product
- Packaging
- Warranty
- Price

- Payment items
- List price
- Leasing options
- Bundling
- Discounts
- Place
- Locations
- Distribution channels
- Logistics and supply
- Channel motivations
- Promotions
- Public relations
- Projected results of the promotional program
- Advertising
- Budget including your break point
- Promotional programs

#7: Short and long term projections

This part should include your break-even analysis, forecast of expenses and revenues and any changes that you predict that you will require in future

#8: The conclusion

This should be an expanded version of the executive summary. Ensure you include all the specific numbers (profits, projected quotes, revenues etc.)

The benefits of the marketing plan

1. Chart to success: Plans are always imperfect things, but if you don't plan, then you are doomed. An inaccurate plan is even better than no plan at all.
2. Rallying point: your plan grants your troops something to rally behind. You want them to feel confident that the captain of the vessel has the charts in order and knows how to steer the ship and has a port of destination in mind.
3. Top level reflection: Given all the activities involved in the operations of the business, it's difficult to turn your attention to the big picture, especially to parts that are not directly associated with the daily operations.
4. Company operational instructions. Marketing plan is a step by step description of your company's success. It's more important than your vision statement. Try to obtain an all-round and genuine marketing plan, so that you could review your company from top to the bottom and ensure all pieces are working well together
5. Captured thinking: Don't allow your financial people to keep numbers in their heads. Financial reports are the essence of any business. Your written documents outline your game plan. Even if people leave or enter the business, the information in the marketing plan should stay intact to remind you of what you had settled upon.

Ideally, after creating your marketing plans for some few years, you can just sit back and check the progress of the company. It might be hard to find time for the review but this could provide an unparalleled and objective view of the business life over some years.

UNIT 4
BRICK AND MORTAR MARKETING

Brick-and-mortar marketing refers to the marketing steps used by companies serving customers directly and face-to-face, often at a storefront. The name was invented in 1992 to give it a more physical aspect.

Purpose

Before beginning any advertising campaign, you have to create a marketing goal, define what you want to sell, why you want to sell it and what differentiates you from your competitors. One of the most common activities employed in this practice is public relations and advertising. They are used to make targeted customers aware of your business. You have to answer many 'why?' questions when marketing your products or services. You should actually think of it as educating yourself. Pretend like you did not know your business existed. This will serve as an excellent marketing campaign that wouldhelp to drive more customers to your business.

Emphasizing Benefits

The advantage of buying from a physical store location is what separates a brick-and-mortar company from any other type of business. Even though people would prefer the convenience of the internet, the physical shopping experience is still very much alive. This is where store-based promotions come into play, not only do they advertise their prices, quality and service; they also promote the location of the store and the unique attributes of personal shopping. Most people love the fact that you can try out products in real-time and communicate directly with the staff. This helps them to select exactly what they need, which in turn offers an enormous advantage to storefront businesses.

Promotions

Even though both online and brick-and-mortar businesses provide discounts and sales promotions, the latter could usually combine strategy with promotions and sales events. Some companies like fashion retailers hold limited-time sales as a way to bring people to their stores, other retailers prefer to hold fewer but major promotional events to draw in bigger crowds. Foot traffic is usually caused when people are walking through the streets, malls and even offices, so when these businesses decide to make events, it often attracts onlookers.

Sales

Sales are a major element of the marketing process for brick-and-mortar stores. In these types of stores, it is usually a team effort since the staffs combine all their hard work to get sales going. Most buyers like this sort of customer experience and often prefer to be swayed instead of picking what they want online. Advantage of having sales teams in brick-and-mortar stores is that the staff can persuade customers to join loyalty programmes, which in turn would promote full customer participation unlike transactions where the customer can just click on the "close' button. Such loyalty programmes help with the collection of critical data from client. This allows the store to use that information in future marketing strategies.

Physical

The physical aspects of a brick-and-mortar business are there for everyone to see, but to increase the likelihood of passers-by entering, quality signage is needed. It must express all the vital elements of the business and reflect its true brand. If you include various signs for different aspects such as "Sales, it is vital that you differentiate them. It is also essential that you attract people when a sale is ongoing because it allows potential customers to know what's going on before entering.

Neighborhood

Marketing in your area can be done using various methods and processes. Some brick-and-mortar businesses use small marketing ads to target close by neighbors, while others volunteer with local neighbors for charity and community organizations to gain trust and visibility. Some companies build partnerships with local schools and communities to create events and promotions; this is highly effective depending on the execution.

Citywide

To reach citywide markets, local advertising in radio stations, area magazines and newspapers is a must. It can provide the exposure you need in your town. One of the fundamental aspects of city marketing is where you place yourself. Personally being a member of various city groups such as the chamber of commerce and city communities would raise your chances of success. In addition, you can also provide word-of-mouth coverage to your city friends and also ask your friendly non-competitive business friends to give their clients a good word about you.

Online

Due to the extreme power of internet searches, it is important that you utilize online resources when marketing your brick-and-mortar business. There are various avenues where you can include your company, some of which include Foursquare, Google Places, and Yelp. In addition, creating an online presence by having a website will allow you to generate interest outside your locality, therefore expanding your reach.

Social Media

Social media can be the best thing that ever happened to your brick-and-mortar business. When creating social media pages such as Facebook and Twitter, interesting content is shared that could engage potential customers. Try to find people who are in your locality by searching for them on social media. Getting more 'followers' and 'likes' puts you in the driving seat to explain to clients what your business is all about. Another beautiful aspect of social media is it allows you to conduct surveys and even address customer service issues. Due to the high number of technologically based users, customers are more likely to explain their problems online. Having a great way of handling customer issues may lead to a positive word-of-mouth marketing.

Customer Service

Continuing with the advantages of customer service, 74% of clients purchase more products based on commercial recommendations. When you provide top class customer service through a quality sales team, it will lead to more returns.

Depending on the type of marketing, you want to do, you will need both an online or offline marketing strategy. Today's brick-and-mortar marketers must not only know how to sell, they must also integrate online and offline marketing tactics to have an advantage over their competitors.

When opening a brick-and-mortar business, you already know it will cost more than an online business, so your marketing plan must be very good. It should be sustainable, achievable and affordable. Finding a way to assimilate all of these techniques will put you in good stead, so try to figure out an effective marketing process as soon as you can.

UNIT 5
ONLINE MARKETING

Today almost every business, regardless of its size, has a website online. Businesses now enjoy the convenience and can also give customers what they want by having a sound presence online. However, having a website isn't enough anymore especially if you want to maximize your success. You need to learn how to successfully market your business online by improving your website's visibility and exposure as a way of generating more online traffic and increasing sales.

Optimize Your Site's Copy For Search Engines

The importance of search engine optimization in the industry today cannot be underestimated. The idea is to develop website content that will rank your site higher on page results of the major search engines like Google, Yahoo and Bing when users perform specific keyword searches. Hundreds of marketing companies specialize in SEO but you can also try a little SEO yourself. Just think of few words or phrases that customers might use when searching for businesses like yours and then type them into the free Google Keyword Tool. You will receive a handful of similar results with few words or longer phrases that you can use in your website copy without actually overdoing it.

Use Pay-Per-Click Advertising

This is often lumped with SEO as a traffic building tool online but it is actually very different. With Pay-per-click you can buy specific keywords and phrases from search engines on a Pay-per-click basis. Depending on the type of business, whenever you purchase a related keyword phrase an ad for your website will appear in the paid results section of any search engine using this phrase. Whenever a user clicks on a link on your ad, you will pay a negotiated fee to the search engine.

Publish an E-Newsletter

Electronic newsletters are one of the most effective ways of driving qualified traffic to your online business. If done properly, you will reach customers and prospects consistently and direct them to your website for a more detailed information about your company, products and services. They are simple and inexpensive to publish but for them to boost your marketing campaign, you have to carefully build your site and also provide valuable content instead of a thinly disguised sales pitch. Also make it easy for subscribers to opt out if they no longer want to receive your e-newsletters.

Write A Blog

Blogging is another effective way of driving qualified traffic to your website and improve your website's ranking in the search engines. You can use blogs to add more keyword phrase pages to your site because search engines view blog posts the same way as they do other web pages. Even if you are unsure about what to write about, don't hesitate to start blogging. You are obviously an expert at something otherwise you won't be running a business. Therefore, think about trends and current happenings in your industry, blog about it to keep your existing customers and prospects informed.

Use Link Exchanges

To determine search results rankings, search engine analytics usually consider the number of links that come into and out of your website popularly known as inbound and outbound links. Link building is therefore a potentially effective tool for driving traffic to your site. Though you can build inbound and outbound links to your website manually, this is a cumbersome and time-consuming process. To increase efficiency, there are online services that can help automate the process making it easy to build reciprocal and one-way links.

Participate In Social Media

Many online social media platforms primarily started off for personal socializing purposes but businesses quickly started using these platforms to drive traffic to their websites. Though creating a coordinated social media and website traffic building strategy for your business is a huge task, you can still manage it or hire professionals to handle it instead. You can create a business Facebook page or a comprehensive LinkedIn profile page, each with links back to your business' website.

The Site Should Be Professional

Your website should be professional in how it looks and reads. A poorly-developed site would stand out but for all the wrong reasons. While it is easier to use free templates like WordPress to build your own site, still consider hiring a professional website designer and copywriter. Primarily, this however depends on two factors, the complexity or the role of your website and your technical proficiency. For an e-commerce website, hire an expert developer but if your site is more of an online marketing tool, try and do it yourself if you have some technical proficiency.

The Site Should Load Quickly And Easily

A common mistake that many businesses online make is building fancy yet slow websites that take ages to load. Besides, research shows that typical users will wait no longer that 2 to 4 seconds for a site to load before giving up and moving on to another. Try and keep the key elements of your website relatively simple unless you are operating a high-tech business and you need to impress visitors with a lot of flash and dash. Your site should load quickly regardless of the type of internet connection a user has. Keep the navigation smooth and easy too so that visitors can quickly access pages on your site.

Generate Positive Customer Reviews

Shoppers to web-based businesses are increasingly relying on customer reviews when deciding which companies to do businesses with. Based on positive or negative reviews of a company, its products and services, customers can choose a provider to buy from. Therefore, generate positive customer reviews by delivering high quality products and an excellent service to all your customers. Always visit authoritative review sites to see what your customers are saying about you and if there are criticisms, post a response quickly.

Keep social media interactions meaningful and considerate without misusing them and creating a general annoyance. Always see your fans and followers as people first, customers second. Make your interactions with them as humanly as possible taking an interest in them. Don't assume that because you are selling, this is the only thing you should concentrate on. Also provide meaningful content that matters to your followers making sure that everything you share resonates with what they like. Link with people and organizations to expose your brand to a larger audience online and also be knowledgeable rather than jump bandwagons. If your employees are representing you on social media, make sure they understand what it means to connect and interact with others online. Also learn from errors made in the past and remember that lack of motivation can derail all your previous efforts as you market your business online.

UNIT 6
ADVERTISING

Advertising services are an absolute essential for a product to compete in the market. It provides a stepping-stone by catering to a wider audience and also aids in creating a brand identity among existing products/services. Marketing is the tool through which a business makes an entry into the market, whereas advertising introduces the product as well as services to the end user.

Another purpose of advertising are to deliver products and services to prospective buyers in an efficient and persuasive manner. The objective of publicity is to grow awareness of a product or service and to build a unique corporate image for an advertiser. Advertising services may consist of market surveys, logo designing, designing brochures and pamphlets, etc. The complete package of initiating effective strategies, attracting customers and promoting events in the print, electronic, radio and online media, lies with the advertising agencies.

Some marketing agencies integrate marketing, branding, and client retention strategies in an attempt to differentiate products and the services provided by an enterprise. These include fermenting marketing strategy, market and product development, customer holding programs, corporate image management, brand strategies, and tailored training in sales, marketing, and business leadership.

Majority of the successful trading and manufacturing companies worldwide have the most dependable advertising strategies that keep their trade volumes on top of the market. How are they achieving this? If you are an entrepreneur who wants to succeed with promotional activities, you need have enough knowledge about types of advertising so that you will be in a position to take advantage of their benefits.

Advertising may be very costly if you are not able to do it right the first time. Of course, if it is not correctly implemented, there is a higher risk for the technique not to work, this is the last thing that you would want to happen. This is the reason this phase may include risks - risks that most small companies would not wish to undertake because it may cause their capitals to deplete. However, in doing business, risks are always present and taking the challenge to face them is actually a part of the game. Below are the categories of advertising that will help you succeed.

The first category of advertising is building your business name and image. If you are just opening your business, it is recommended that you pick an appealing name that may best describe what your company is all about. Keep in mind, there are some businesses that offer the same goods as your business and having a noble company image and name will help you stand out from the rest.

Another category of advertising is branding your product. It is essential that your label, just like your business name, is outstanding and could easily be remembered by people. If you are a new entrant, there are already established brands in the market and you must attempt required to outshine them. This is why branding is critical.

Performing a promotional campaign. This is harder to do for a service than a product as there is no tangible product. You would need to give details, illustrate and demonstrate how your business works.

If your firm does not want to interact with the public, there is no need to consider television and radio promotions. It would be better to engage potential customers through direct mail or by placing print ads in different publications.

If you are just starting a small business, it will be beneficial to participate in Co-op advertising wherein you absorb a portion of the cost and supply the necessary artwork for the advertising campaign. By doing this, you share the expenses with another company.

Another option is going into public service advertising where you can do promotions in a positive light which is also a better way of building your image.

Knowing what sort of advertising to use in your business is one way of reducing your operating expenses. It may be helpful to conduct a study or analysis first before crafting your marketing process plan and advertising methods so that you could evaluate if the execution would return a positive outcome. There should be no room for errors because second chances would result in more costs. Thus, it is best to get it correct the first time!

Benefits Of Successful Advertising

What is the secret to more successful advertising? It is not about giving an adverting agency plenty of money for to do something intelligent and creative. Is it not about having sexy models with witty catch-phrases or fancy photography. No! Advertising, whether it's done using a computer, in print or via the airwaves, is about making successful sales pitches and persuading clients to purchase an item. That is the whole notion of advertising in few words.

The most significant thing to remember about your consumers or clients is this: they're not interested in the precise features of a product or service or in it's price. As hard as this is to believe, they're not concerned about supporting you or your business! All clients, whether they realize or acknowledge it or not, really want one thing: BENEFITS! They want the benefits that products and services could provide to improve the quality of their lives.

UNIT 7
MASS MEDIA

The advent of social media has completely revolutionized the way marketing is done. However, individuals, government agencies, corporations, and non-profit organizations still use various channels (besides traditional media) of communication to reach their target audience. Traditional marketing/ communication channels, such as television (TV) and radio, play a major role in advertising. Other forms include newspapers, magazines, and the Internet. Organizations create ad campaigns that typically rely on one or many of these.

The Function of Radio, Television, and Other Media in Marketing

Outreach
The major advantage TV ads offer is 'outreach.' National television, for instance, has a larger audience. Despite criticisms for its inherent high costs, advertisers out to reach a large audience have the best chance to accomplish this through television. Fundamentally, reach can be defined as the total number of people typically exposed to an advertising message. Because of this, television is often used by companies or organizations focused on generating brand awareness as one of their main objective.

Deliver Creativity
TV offers some of the greatest creative opportunities among

traditional media. It combines audio and visual elements to form dynamic stories. Advertisers tell a story within their ads to have an impact on their target audience. Creativity adds greater meaning to company brands beyond the basic products or services. Through TV, which offers multi-sensory appeal, advertisers have the advantage of creating emotional connections by incorporating characters that the target audience can be able to relate to.

Radio Costs

Radio, as a media communication channel, is ideally one of the inexpensive traditional media. Commercial radio stations sell "airtime" to advertisers to generate their revenue. Because radio requires no video equipment and logistics, like the expensive television commercials (which can also be tedious to produce), most small businesses prefer to use radio to reach their audience. This is because radio spots – often sold in bundles of a particular number of spots (rotational) – are less costly than TV placement.

In deciding which advertising media to go for, a business has to consider several aspects, including the cost of advertising. In fact, a budget largely influences the decision on what advertising channel to use. Radio is often chosen when a company operating on a shoestring budget wants to reach a larger audience. But unfortunately, the painful truth is that even with a massive advertising budget, this channel poses a great challenge in creating memorable advertising.

Relative impact of various advertising media

- Direct Mail: Of all media, it has the highest impact, and the message reaches each intended recipient in a much more personalized manner, and at the time the audience has chosen to consider that particular message. It can be the most effective, although the cost of reaching one customer via direct mail can be greater than TV.
- Television: Presents the advertiser with an opportunity to communicate to a captive audience, as viewers are more apt to tune into an ad, though the cost of buying a spot can be greater than other media like radio.
- Radio: Presents a great improvement over print ads, as the listeners are captive to your message, unless their radio is turned off or they decide to switch the station. The cost expended to reach the same magnitude as that of a print ad may be higher.
- Newspapers – typically the cheapest way of reaching a mass audience, but with many ads, tiny ads often get lost in the visual clutter, as readers simply scan newspapers.
- Magazines: The opportunity presented to capture the reader's attention is a bit higher, as readers tend to scan or peruse magazines more keenly than they do newspapers. This is because ads placed there are fewer per page. Compared to newspaper ads, magazine ads often cost more.

6: Social media: The advent of social media has made advertising relatively cheaper for smaller businesses that may "pay per click" or per day. They are used to target a specific audience within a given budget.

Therefore, unless you have a hefty budget to make it memorable, it is advisable to always try one advertising medium at a time. However, keep in mind that while one medium may work very well for one product or service, the same medium can be a total failure for another. Marketing managers must understand that there are many variables that could impact the outcome of an advertising campaign before spending millions of their company's dollars on any particular one. By first testing the effectiveness of a message in select media, they can find the most appropriate vehicle or channel for promoting the company brand or product. While many debate whether advertising is an art or a science, the ability to find a balance between the two can make all the difference.

UNIT 8
CUSTOMER RELATIONSHIP MANAGEMENT

In markets where high competition prevails, it is important for each business to develop a positive association with its clients and customers. Whether it is a small scale business or a global e-commerce, it has become a necessity to establish a healthy relationship with existing customers to ensure that they come back for more. This will also generate new leads and would help the business entity attract new customers and increase its customer base. Another advantage is that customer reviews highlight the preferences of commodities and services prevailing in the current market and indicate what could be done to enhance sales.

What is Customer relationship management?

To put more emphasis on the business, it is really important that the demands and needs of the customers are studied well. This way the business entity would be able to adapt itself according to the varied needs and preferences of different customers.

Why use Customer relationship management?

To expand a business, evolution and adaptation are of great importance. It is in the best interest of the business entity that it continues doing business with its existing customers and in the same time welcome more customers. Good customer relationship management produces the following results:

- Better understanding of customers
- More efficient service to customers
- Anticipation of customers' needs and wants

This will, in turn work, towards achieving greater customer satisfaction, decreasing operational cost, increasing staff productivity and the effectiveness of each customer interaction.

How does it work?

Customer relationship management is no more than a business strategy. The sole aim of this strategy is to uplift the prospects for a business entity, through maintaining a healthy and positive relationship with its customers. Businesses are able to plan their future aspects and make policies accordingly.

Customers are the backbone of any business. In today's tech savvy world, maintaining customer details manually is of no use and can be considered a waste of time. It is important that all customer details are recorded accurately and in a timely manner. The Customer relationship management software does the work of instantly creating and saving the details of new and existing customers. This information can be accessed at any point in time, thereby increasing the accuracy and ease of monitoring customers.

Customer Relationship Management (CRM) Software

Customer Relationship Management software is now available in various packages, each with distinctive features. Some of the popular CRMs are Sage customer relationship management, Sage SalesLogix and Microsoft Dynamics Customer relationship management.

Choosing a right Customer relationship management provider is as important as choosing the appropriate software. Since you will be binding with the service provider for a long term, it is important that you check all the aspects and services that are being provided by the Customer relationship management service provider.

UNIT 9
BUDGETING

One of the most critical elements of running a modern enterprise is managing the finances of the company. One of the key areas of concern is the marketing budget. This budget line can bleed cash out of the company faster than sales can keep up. Whether the company is a multimillion-dollar enterprise or a new start-up running on bootstrapping principles, the name of the game is the same- the company must moniter its cash flow. This section addresses how budgeting works in marketing and shows how an enterprise can manage its budgets while achieving its marketing objectives.

WHO IS RESPONSIBLE FOR THE MARKETING BUDGET?

Before delving into the nitty-gritties of a marketing budget, it is important to assign responsibilities for the marketing budget. The model presented here is for a mid-sized company and may vary according to the size of the organization. The person who bears the most responsibility for the marketing budget is the Marketing Manager or the person who answers for the performance of the marketing department. In many cases, the marketing manager will be the one to propose what needs to be done, and to give an estimate of how much is needed. The marketing manager may report directly to a board, the CEO, or the Vice President of marketing. This means that this person (or group) shares in the responsibility of analyzing and approving the marketing budget estimates prepared by the marketing manager. Apart from these, the marketing team plays a crucial role in the development of the marketing budget. This team has a front-line understanding of the needs of the company, and is charged with implementing the strategy adopted by the board.

IMPORTANCE OF MARKETING BUDGETS

Marketing budgets play three critical roles in an organization. Firstly, the budget forces the marketing manager to prioritize expenses. As noted earlier, uncontrolled expenditure on marketing can make a company bleed cash fast. A marketing manager needs to take into account the total revenues of the company and make a budget that fits within the financial abilities of the company. If there is need to spend sums above what the company currently controls, then the manager must justify this position and should indicate where the company can obtaine the extra resources needed to fund the marketing budget. In this sense, a marketing budget forces a marketing manager to choose budget items that the company can afford.

Secondly, marketing budgets help companies to allocate sufficient funds for marketing. The whole point of making a budget is to have a preview of what it would cost a business unit to achieve its goals. Chances are the management team gave the marketing manager certain goals for marketing. This means that the marketing manager must come up with a set of proposals on how to meet these targets. If a company wants to gain market share, the marketing needs differ from a situation where the company wants to maintain its market share. The marketing manager must get the ideal balance between the most effective marketing approach, and the least expensive methods of achieving marketing targets. In this sense, a marketing budget ensures that the marketing manager has sufficient resources to deliver the targets set by the board. Note that the budget should be just enough to cover projected expenses and not more than what is actually needed. A separate contingency fund can handle marketing contingencies and can be used to take advantage of unforeseen marketing opportunities.

Thirdly, marketing budgets provide a basis for reviewing the performance of a marketing campaign. When evaluating the performance of the company in a given period, or when reviewing the performance of a particular marketing campaign, it is important to compare achieved results with the invested resources. If a marketing campaign cost $100,000 then the company should be able to tell whether there was a good return on this investment. Did sales go up? Did market share grow? Did revenues increase because of this campaign? In addition, when the company is reporting to its shareholders, the marketing budget can be the basis for providing analysis on the effectiveness of the business strategy currently employed by the firm.

PROCESS OF BUDGETING IN MARKETING

The process of budgeting in marketing is not constant, and cannot be standardized across all organizations. It is dependent on the organizational structure, ownership structure, legal considerations, size of the organization and even its geographical location. The following elements illustrate some of the fundamental processes involved in setting a marketing budget.

Firstly, each company needs to develop a set of marketing objectives. In some companies, the board or the CEO may be the most appropriate person to create the marketing strategy. However, the marketing manager could develop the objectives.

Secondly, the company must identify its marketing priorities. This may be characterized as specific goals, or may be a general statements showing what the company needs to do in order to achieve its marketing objectives. If the overall objective of the marketing campaign is to increase market share, then the priorities in the marketing strategy could include winning existing customers currently served by competitors or venturing into new market segments currently not served by the company.

The third stage involves identifying appropriate marketing channels to achieve the stated objectives. This stage will lead to the development of detailed expense items and will be the basis for the budget.

Finally, the company needs to rationalize the marketing budget alongside all its other budgets to ensure it has the financial muscle to handle all its commitments. It may be possible to arrive at a budget quota for marketing before starting the detailed budgeting process based on the overall financial health of the company and its overall business objectives. This approach ensures all departments get some financing, but it may limit the potential of other departments.

www.ingramcontent.com/pod-product-compliance
Lightning Source LLC
Chambersburg PA
CBHW071830200526
45169CB00018B/1306